Scott J. Schiappacasse resides in Skokie, Illinois. He is the youngest of seven children. He has been living with Bipolar Disorder since his late teenage years and writing poetry is one of his coping strategies. Not only does his poetry provide him solace, it provides comfort to others as well. Scott is an active member of his church where he has done some poetry readings. He has written several poetry books that he hopes to release to the general public after this current one.

I find nature walks with friends very healing and
inspiring.

Scott J. Schiappacasse

NO LOST TEARS

A Collection of Poetry

AUSTIN MACAULEY PUBLISHERS™
LONDON • CAMBRIDGE • NEW YORK • SHARJAH

Ordering Information
Quantity sales: Special discounts are available on quantity purchases by corporations, associations, and others. For details, contact the publisher at the address below.

Publisher's Cataloging-in-Publication data
Schiappacasse, Scott J.
No Lost Tears

ISBN 9798889107323 (Paperback)
ISBN 9798889107330 (ePub e-book)

Library of Congress Control Number: 2023924474

www.austinmacauley.com/us

First Published 2024
Austin Macauley Publishers LLC
40 Wall Street, 33rd Floor, Suite 3302
New York, NY 10005
USA

mail-usa@austinmacauley.com
+1 (646) 5125767

I would like to thank Laura Gerber, PhD for kickstarting my desire to publish, writing the author's bio and keeping tabs on me after my parents passed.

Barnum & Bailey

Barnum & Bailey
And goofin' around

Clownin' not frownin'
From town to town

Glitters of glee
Spreadin' the glow

Teeth all so happy
Depression a no.

Takin' the idea
Of seeing the glee

Takin' it home
With you and
With me.

Basically

Basically I'm waiting
For the next creating.

Basically I'm in pain,
Growing into the gain.

Basically I cycle quickly,
Like the sun to the moon.

Basically I do my best,
To make life lest the pest.

Basically I feel better,
When others feel better.

Basically I understand
And yet am mystified.

Basically I am blinded,
& yet see all too well.

Basically.

Blooms of Hope

How many of us
Suffer in silence?

Waiting for that
Next bloom of hope.

Trying to ignore the
Reoccurring pains.

Not wanting others
To know our private strain.

We laugh together in
Those blooms of hope.

God is the only one
Willing to listen.

And the only one we
Care to share with.

Good Grief

I dragged the sand bags, finally
Surrounding the stain glass.

It shattered anyway,
Where was I now?

Nowhere to be found,
I walked blindly onward.

Carefully I waited,
Prayers kept traveling.

Color me a rainbow, a
Pot of gold is somewhere,

How can a destroyed person
Still exist? This mystifies me

I never knew what you
Went through, I swear.

Invisible Tears

Tears of joy and sadness,
Running down my face.

They are not visible
Yet they are there.

I may not seem to care,
Yet I am there, carefully.

Do you have these tears?
Running down your face?

Mysteriously invisible
Yet strangely evident.

How does one deal
With invisible tears?

What do they mean
Really mean to one?

No Lost Tears

As I cry myself to sleep,
I enter a world of quality.

My heart teaches me that,
My tears are kept closely.

I awake with strength &
Imaginations full of hope.

My tears were prayers,
Not understood by me.

Running like a child,
In sheer glee & happiness.

Like a lion I move into,
The sunrises of tomorrows.

Musically I stand in the winds,
Of perfumes of true rainbows.

Nothingness

Nothing, nothingness,
Inside of this cloud.

Empty emptiness,
This silence is loud.

I stumble as I begin to rise,
Wiping away all of the lies.

A tunnel through a mountain,
Will end at a great fountain.

I will laugh once again,
Shaking off all the sins.

Others have made it here too.
Made it all the way through.

My smile has joined me once more.
My wings now have winds to soar.

Drenched in Happiness

The creation power of life is always around.
I want the wisdom it holds. Please give that wisdom
That I will not lose so that I may love like I should.
I want to see all that there is through wisdom's
Eyes, drenched in happiness from this newfound

Vision. Peace will be the fruit. Graceful, dancing
Wind sees my cry as it leaves my lips. Hope is born
Looking like a tree sprout bursting out of the
Ground.

Hope is...

Hope is a flower of steel and of gold.
It's bright as the sun,

I must focus on this, oh, so old,

It's ancient and new,
Now and always,

A sight to be seen,
Kindness and patience,

And wisdom within,
This thing called hope,

A compass, a guide,
A conscience, not strife.

Peace in the turmoil,
Thank God for this flame,

Called hope.

Miracles?

Flowers from seeds.
Fields from rain.

Freedom from pain.
Good feelings unseen.

What's the use?

Hope keeps,
Coming along.
Singing its song.

Cheering me up,
Once again.

Can't deny it,
Everyone's tried it.

Come on,
Come clean.

Candles

Shining, glowing,
Showing, guiding.

Happiness is not
A mere holiday.

But a bundle,
Kept in the
Heart of
All who will.

Capturing this firefly,
In the heart's jar,

Feeding it with
Memories and
Hope-filled dreams.

Finding life & joy
In the now.

Pouring

Pouring over pages,

Pouring over me.

Strength is growing
Stronger.

Creating a certain
Glee.

Quite a puzzling
Vision.

Clarity is claiming
Me.

Albatross

Unwanted, uncared for, unseen
Potential cast aside.
Jesus sees this travesty,
Why must this trash-talk rule
Press on? Good will come.

I wade in what I don't know.
Truth, peace, wisdom
Paves paths of gold.

Righteousness is not
An ideal but a happiness
Realized in the midst.

I grow in pain sometimes.
I wait for the fruits of labor.
There will be the unseen.

The contentment
Can always be now.
This garbage can is
Merely a treasure chest.
Oh blind one, please see.
I wait. Will you?

In the Icy Waters

In the icy waters I
Swim to the shore.

Darting on the land to
The beach towel that

Is warmed by the hot
Sun & sand, still shivering

I wonder what
I was thinking to dive

Off that pier. My senses
Now very alive & alert

I lie down and get lost
Into an old dusty book.

Changes

I wait for you to change,
And change I will and do.

Learning, growing, waiting,
Dreaming, hoping, caring.

Grasping, climbing, clinging,
Over mountainsides I go.

Pages, prayers, presentations,
Listening, sensing, observations.

Soldiers made of conscience,
Come with hearts of gold.

Will we leave the hollow gaze or,
Nimbly travel through a maze?

Stunned we've traveled this far,
Looking back, astounding ourselves.

Dismal Nights

Dismal nights,
Dazzling dawns.

Waiting for the
Night to pass.

Sleep avoids me,
Like a stranger.

Poetry is my
Quiet friend.

My heart needs
No more sadness.

Will I sleep
Or will I toss?

Hope draws nearer
Like the new dawn.

Power Line

Have you felt alive
Like a power line?

Can't take the credit
Better than ourselves.

Ideas from another.
Creative, aware, alive.

Amazed by all the travels.
Yet we are still intact.

Give some love away.
Best advice I can give.

Priceless

As precious jewelry
My parents were

Priceless. I long
For conversations

That have not
Been replicated.

For connection
That has not

Been matched
I will plug along.

Puzzles in Waiting

Unending puzzles of importance.
Unwinding in waiting rooms.

Darkness for this bird's cage.
Sleeping for another morrow.

Abstracts make sense somehow.
A tussle in a restful state.

Planets speeding in circles.
Stars glowing in darkness.

Flitting about on the flip side.
Perching for a moment of rest.

To Gratefulness

Whether it be this or that,
The other thing or whatever.

Gratefulness comes in handy.
I have too often & too soon,

Forgot my many blessings,
I am not alone in this curse.

It steals from my contentment,
Also causes some resentment,

Instead of enjoying moments,
In my journey, not just goals.

May patience be given to me
Without thorns of perplexity.

May I speed into virtues/values
With the payment of graces.

Trouble Comes

Trouble comes and trouble goes.
Waiting for the storm to pass.

Internal storms of greater mass.
Outward signs show no mess.

Jesus, quietly hold me near.
Will I let go of all the fear.

Fragile bodies hold this storm.
Is always the forever norm.

Trouble comes and trouble goes.
Grinding us like a scented rose.

Worlds Inside

Worlds inside this stamp
Inside this a little lamp

Give light to a dusty table.
Written on it a little fable

About a wagon in decay &
A mouse refusing to stay.

Tumble weeds blowing.
Wildflowers growing.

This stamp I mail today.
On this very ordinary day.

Crumbling Christmas

Once a golden state of mind,
Then a crumbling Christmas.

Parents loving always found,
Then a crumbling Christmas.

Friends and church come aglow.
Filled my heart to overflow.

Began to mend my broken heart,
Gave me reason a new start.

No longer a crumbling season.
Love breathes quietly in me.

Easter Morning

As flowers burst from the snow,
So, my heart rises from death.

On this holy day of Easter,
I now take my first breath.

Like a bridge from nothing,
To a land of great promise.

I can now walk in clouds
Of better love and peace.

Joy is at my door and also,
Great rewards hold me close.

Engraved on My Heart

Two of one, called parents.
Etched on my life forever.

Lessons by example & voice.
Sacrifice done by choice.

Gives and gives again to me.
Day after day creates a glee.

Realizing more what was meant.
Not ever perfect but was love.

Now I turn to scripture to see.
What they pulled upon for me.

Enjoying the Unravel

As I unwittingly unravel,
Trying to enjoy the travel.

Waiting on sent prayers,
Calming any risen fears.

Not responsible for it all.
Doing my best that is all.

Needing better foresight,
Even though I'm all right.

Knowing there is a God.
Knowing I am not him.

Glad to See Joy

Glad to see you
A light so bright,

In my heart today.
Did nearly miss,

This morning kiss,
Being laughed away.

Floats down as snow,
On breezes, it flows.

Touches down softly
On tulips blooming.

Pain Ting

No pain for this soldier yet
Cause for distress in redress.

Cancelation in redirection,
Waiting, writing, bleeding.

From the thorns of truth,
That I hand in full to you.

Somewhere a calm will be,
In our midst in a forever.

While with this fever,
I can only be forgotten.

Puzzle Piece Made of Tangles

Puzzle piece made of tangles,
While working all these angles.

Untangling all the perplexities &
Finding where this piece does fit.

While holding back the storm's floods,
And learning to realize some patience.

Are the tangles glued confusions,
Or perplexities with unknown answers?

My perspectives are limited wishing prayers.
Also using clarity from friends & brothers.

Chocolates

Bitter-sweet Valentine
Will you be fully mine?

Don't hate this circus,
That we've designed.

So lived and so divine.
We are mere mortals.

You are the only vine.
Feebly, I walk the line.

Forgive me as I am,
Riddled with errors.

Drama Spills

Spinning into the breeze,
I fall into another breath,

Fall into another death.
What will become of me?

Will I fight or will I flee?
Can I stand? Can I bleed?

Drama spills from this cup.
No matter what, this I know…

This is mine, to search & find,
For better days & finer truths.

Purpose Bubble

Gliding into a better day.
Then falling far, far away.

Up to be a better you.
Down you go, must not be true.

Nothing points me in no way.
Pointless ways in every day.

Gifted me without a God.
Does no good; I only rot.

Pushing into a purpose bubble,
Keeps me strong, out of trouble.

Reflections

Pondering viewpoints,
Creating a new point.

Standing still over again,
Seeing new ways of ability.

Building 3D vision clarity.
Strengthening heart with hilarity.

Knowing & knowing & knowing
Life can be truly shalom for me.

From outside and inside
Quality is granted.

God sustains our breath.
Our greatness has humility

Swimming in ocean's depth,
Flying through space & time.

The Mouse That Roared

If I can't love you who I see,
How can I love in eternity?

I let go of my grudge before
It gains a stench of death.

Stepping over every offense,
Looking past their ugliness.

Mercies given for my cause.
Mercies tied up in these laws.

Silently this mouse will roar,
To pull a thorn to love me.

To Be

I fall asleep in fear
To wake in your care

Chains are but dust,
In love and not lust.

To see again with eyes
Through this disguise.

I can, I cannot begin,
To end humor's sin.

Will I do this for you
To tell you what's true.

Immortal

Wait no longer, my breath.
Seeing the end, this death.

Her face reflects my hope.
I fall endlessly into the eyes

In but a moment you win me.
Stealing sanity, giving clarity.

I walk inside my thoughts now.
To pen a verse as I rehearse.

The story we live & experience
Never ends but does it begin.

Care Fully

Dizzy with the spin of illness.
I then fly over my dark spells.

I am chained to this dungeon.
Then with wings into sunlight.

Clarity steals me from my pain.
My heart is full of quality Hope.

Press in, press on, a soul's wish.
Speak as if it were you, soldier.

As one has said well to my ears,
"A wise man measures his words."

Tamed and Bridled

Tornados of my misery,
Breaking into splinters.

Tears on war torn men,
Taming this inner hell.

Bridling it for service,
To right the wrongs,

Of my misperceptions.
Sleep, sleep & dream.

Will we walk together
In this new found light.

Hear My Prayer

I was alone, just me.
Silent ability hides.

Bind my shadows,
So I see what waits.

Needing to see me.
Not just perplexity,

A bliss of no value.
Free my emotions.

In a perfect world,
The stoic ways end.

Fog of Distress

Paralyzes me into a boredom,
I try to unmask it, to re task it.

This burp is a change for me,
Seems like a mountain I see.

Blinds my future plans to be.
We push at this bag of terror.

Now this wave spills over me,
A calm, a peace, a reprieve.

An aid of grace in my corner.
Time heals, heals, and heals.

Reflecting in these mirrors,
These people of kindness.

Touch the Clouds

I fall again from the spin,
I turn to Him once again.

Touch the clouds of prayer,
Inside my common language.

He understands my tangles.
A hope arrow into His heart.

A wink from Heaven's gate,
Inside my daily spin of life.

It gives me a spark of Love.
From Father God up above.

Artistic Knots of Clarity

Will we muse the answers?
A tapestry of my spinning.

Fishing with nets, not lines.
A mass appeal for my God.

Crystal-clear this breath.
It'll help me, help you too.

Envision a truth of light.
Patience is given in verse.

I know I will learn, I will.
Goodness can be learned.

Forgiving to Love You

Love is all about a giving & humility.
One way is to walk in forgiveness.
This is part of the Lord's Prayer.

"Forgive us our debts as we
Forgive our debtors."

When offended, you set it aside,
And focus on the real issue.
Knowing that people need love.

When you do this, you create
A bridge to heal the situation.

This is also a way of giving Mercy.
So it will be available for you.

Two other words for walking in
Love are Kindness and Patience.

"When you are kind to others,
You help yourself." Good enough.
Patience is helpful when learned.
Pray for an understanding heart.

Fast

Fasting at last for least,
Of leasing at last to fast.

Twice a twin of thrice,
Of rice to feed the mice.

Drunk to drink the drank,
Spills the spruce of goose.

Cans of candles of can do,
Zips the snippers of zoo.

Fells the trees of knees,
Once to make me sneeze.

Happy Steady Pills

Crystal clarity is my desire
My only fire to free myself.

Making me a real boy from
A heart and smile of wood.

Jesus spins a pill of magic
Splintering the tragic lore.

My inner groan cries for a
New droplet shaping stone.

Only Hope's light shatters
The dark mysteries today.

When Will I

When will I go into your eyes
Of new life to strive to heal

To hope to breathe all at once
The next step for me is life.

A life that lives for all ways
All days, no nights, no death

I will, I will speak to see life.
See a life of love to see love.

A joy now that really matters
I sleep into your love so true.

Got Life

When joy enters your soul,
You tend to be more whole

When happiness is there,
It comes when someone cares

When mercy is for givin',
Life is better livin'

Wipe my tears
And calm my fears

'Cause that's the way
For life.